"With terrifying elegance, *Severed* blurs the lines between violence and desire, casting a spell in which even the tenderest intimacy can feel like a murder, a haunting, a loss of vital self. The play moved me as deeply as it scared me; I felt the cold fingers of a dogmatic past reach for my throat with stunning physical realness. A remarkable work."

-Will Arbery

"What if, looking into a mirror, you saw in the reflection the most distorted, monstrous version of yourself staring back at you? What if, unearthing your innermost longings, you bore witness to the unspeakable carnage wrought by your imagined double? Ignacio Lopez dares to ask these questions in his mesmerizing, unsettling solo piece *Severed*. Lopez excavates the torment of his own coming of age/coming out story while simultaneously inhabiting the nightmarish psyche of one of history's most demonic butchers. *Severed* is a tautly written, unflinching, and beautifully spun meditation on desire, forbidden yearning, guilt, and transcendence."

-Carlos Murillo

T0021768

53 SP 33
November 2020
Brooklyn, NY

Severed
© Ignacio Lopez 2020
53rdstatepress.org

Severed is made possible by the New York State Council on the Arts with the support of Governor Andrew M. Cuomo and the New York State Legislature.

Book design: Kate Kremer

ISBN Number: 978-1732545229
Library of Congress Number: 2020948309

Printed in the United States of America

SEVERED

by Ignacio Lopez

53rd State Press
Brooklyn, NY

For John Salyers and Darryl Mack,
who left us too soon.

CONTENTS

INTRODUCTION

It's terrifying to admit how vulnerable we are. We tend to push away thoughts regarding the fragility of our existence. Personally, I have a lot of fear surrounding mental illness. When my anxiety or depression rears up, I wonder, "What if this was every day?" and even more alarming, "What if it got worse? What if I lost control of my own mind?" On the bad days this doesn't feel like paranoia. It feels like a possible reality a razor's edge away. Sitting with yourself and examining these kinds of fears can be a cold and lonely exercise, and comfort in their wake can be hard to come by.

When I saw Ignacio's play *Severed* performed at the Starr Reading Series, I hadn't read the script so I was hearing it fresh. I remember how it slowly and stealthily started to inch me closer to the idea of my own vulnerability. Oddly, I could feel myself opening up more and more even as the show revealed its increasingly gruesome subject matter. To explain this dichotomy, I look no further than Ignacio, whose natural generosity and empathy is so apparent in his writing that it's hard not to want to meet him there—to open up, to relate, and to examine the things you protect and keep hidden. That sensation, that compulsion to be vulnerable, paired with the play's graphic content, made watching it a harrowing experience. There were moments when I felt myself under its power and wasn't sure if I was actually... safe. But Ignacio always worked in some beautiful piece of humanity to let me know he was still there with me, like a therapist guiding me through a particularly difficult part of analysis, and at the end of the reading I felt the real gift of the show. We had engaged in a communal sharing of what scares us most—our fears of personal disaster, of loneliness, of darkness, of calamity—and then we had walked away from that experience knowing something that actually did bring me comfort. That although there is fear, there is darkness, there is danger, and although we ultimately must walk these paths ourselves, when we share these fears with each other, we are not alone.

-Noel Allain

CHARACTERS

Jeff:

The day before his thirty-third birthday. He speaks into a microphone throughout, his voice amplified. He is giving an interview. He speaks the *italicized text*.

Ignacio:

At age twenty-one, months prior to Jeff's interview, and now, many years later. His voice is unamplified. He speaks the unitalicized text.

One actor plays both roles.

Scene titles and stage directions remain unspoken. Scene titles may be projected in performance or omitted altogether.

(A man stands with his back towards us, a light illuminating his arm, extended and bare. The arm moves slowly, his body still. The arm flexes, twists. The fist clenches and releases. The musculature, the structure, contorts, tenses, relaxes and tightens again, over and over in variations, highlighting its architecture. Sinews and bones. Then, as if it had been cleft from the body, the arm suddenly drops. Quick and complete darkness.)

BIRTH/BREACH

(A gentle light.)

Light danced across my mother's eyes and, for a moment, sweet flowers floated above her face, their fragrance nectar on her lips when she ran her tongue over them. A quick breath in—

(He breathes in.)

—as I was lifted out. A constellation fell out of alignment. In the sky, colors refracted, the skin and veins of her closed eyes a prism. For a moment, there was no sound. No breath. No heart. No world. Only colors of light and a sweet smell, like jasmine at dusk.

It was easy for me.

(He breathes in.)

I was lifted gently out. But there were complications and cesareans were not simple then. Thirty-three years ago they cut you open from side to side.

(He makes a cutting motion across his abdomen.)

They severed muscles that never healed. Recuperation took painful weeks. Natural childbirth was never an option again. And I was born only three hundred and sixty days after my sister. My mother was not ready for another child. I was born long and thin. Like a frog. Undernourished.

My father in the delivery room. The obstetrician, a close family friend. He says to my father, "Alberto, she should not have another baby." My father shakes his head. "Alberto, it could kill her. You should let me." My father won't have it. He's heard this all before. It's my mother's fourth cesarean. "You're such a pessimist," my father says. "If she becomes pregnant again, even if she dies, that's God's will." I see that moment as I am lifted up into the world, and the man who holds me, induces me to breathe and brings me to life ... he speaks to the man who created me as he proudly demonstrates his faith, smiling, confident ... and leaves my mother, lying there unconscious, her body open to the elements ... he leaves her to God.

Now, when my father tells this story, he says, "See, if it was up to your mother, you would never have been born."

Could it have been worse? Could my father have left my mother for long periods, consumed by his work and his desire to be free from all the burdens he knew would come with a family? Could this child have been exactly what he didn't want? Or could it have been something that in his mind once seemed so assumed, so normal—"I'll get married and have some kids"? Wasn't it just supposed to happen? Could it be that he resented the responsibilities as they mounted one on top of the other until he took refuge in seeing himself as the breadwinner, the bill-payer, the worker who stayed out of the house with nothing more asked of him? Could he have left my mother completely alone in a room of her husband's father's house?

Could I, her pregnancy, have left my mother in a state of constant nausea, vomiting for forty weeks—two hundred and eighty days? Could she have become nervous, developing a fear of every little thing? Could noises have set her off, strange sounds from neighbors' apartments, banging in the walls, and cooking odors that made her vomit more, causing constant battles between her and my father? "You have to tell them to stop cooking whatever it is they're cooking." "What do you want me to do, bang on the neighbor's door every night and tell them they can't cook what they want to cook in their own house?" Could it be that she would finally lose control and fits would overcome her—legs locking, body trembling all over?

Could her jaw have seized and locked itself to the right, out of alignment, and her eyes, bulging almost out of her face? Could she have even frothed at the mouth? Could my father, bewildered by the spasms, have tried to soothe her, to walk her around the apartment, trying to loosen her legs, relax her body? Almost holding her up because she couldn't walk? And when that didn't work, when the spasms came more and more frequently and the sounds that came out of the walls and the smells of the neighbors' cooking and all the vomiting . . . could my father have given up, afraid of what might come? Could the doctors have stared in confusion, doctor after doctor, bewildered, until they started injecting her with barbiturates and, after that failed, with morphine? "To be honest, we don't know what's causing these seizures." Until they turned my mother away, sending her home with a bottle of Pheno-barbital, to start, and then more and more bottles, until she was taking twenty-six pills a day?

Drugged, with her seizures finally allayed and body list-less . . . Would my father have returned to his duties, to his office to earn a living, leaving my mother alone from before the crack of dawn had pierced through the darkness of her drugged unconsciousness until early evening, when she had passed out again in the living room chair, living her life under sagging lids, looking out into an empty room for someone she knew should be there but who wouldn't come when she called out to him? "Lionel?" Did she remember that she still had a child inside of her?

(He looks down to his stomach.)

"How did I get so fat?" Or did she wonder what would come out and regret that it would? "You'll wish you never were," or, "I hope you won't be as lonely as me." What would have come out after forty weeks, after two hundred and eighty days of noises and smells and vomiting and bulging eyes and locked legs and frothing mouths and bottles of drugs and complete loneliness? Would it have been me?

ADOLESCENCE/DESCENT

When we were young, my sister and I would play under a large weeping willow in the back of our house. It was at least thirty feet tall or more. We would climb up through its branches—which were broad and knotted, with lots of nooks to put our feet—and climb pretty high. The view was spectacular. We could see out over our roof and down several houses in every direction. For a kid of four or five, that was far. The best part was that we went unseen. A weeping willow's branches end in a cascade of tendrils, ten or fifteen feet long down to the ground and studded their entire length with spaded leaves. The tree casts a tremendous skirt of vines around itself. When you approach it, you draw aside this curtain and, once it's closed behind you, stand under the tree unseen. My sister and I would play there, peeking out through the lattice of vines and leaves, looking over neighbors' fences into yards of people we didn't know. We ran there to hide from punishments. To cry sometimes. It was a quiet place, far away from the world. From high up, I would spy on people. I saw what they did when they thought they were alone. I imagined I could hear what they were thinking, the quiet things they were saying to themselves when no one was watching.

My mother was sick a lot. Depressed. In bed all day. She

was sick so much, Dad had to be both parents for me and my brother. Dad and her fought a lot. We stopped going to church. But we were pretty… happy. Once, me and Dad and our dog, we walked all morning to this farm to get eggs for breakfast, a couple of miles, then walked back. Dad was still driving me out to Barberton on Saturdays for chocolate ice cream sodas. Started doing that when we lived out in Ames.

A lot of it was normal. I was in soccer for a while, tennis, band. Clarinet.

(He chortles.)

Went with the Boy Scouts once to New Mexico. Dad tried to get me into stuff. Took me to his lab once, showed me his projects. Did the acid-base test, where the liquid changes color depending on what you put in: red for acids, blue for bases. Showed me his beakers. Geiger counter.

Dad got me a professional bow and arrow set. Taught me how to shoot in the woods behind our house.

I must have been twelve, thirteen. I don't remember going with him to choose the one I wanted. I remember him calling me into his room. He was sitting on the edge of the bed, holding it in his lap. "Well, what do you think?"

It was all black, with an angled grip. It was cold. Dense. Oily. Very heavy. It left a diamond pattern impression on my hand. It reminded me of the German guns you saw in World War II movies or on *Hogan's Heroes*.

I remember buying bullets with my father. I remember playing with the empty plastic cases. I remember the black zippered pouch with the fuzzy red lining and where my father kept it on his bedside table. I remember the firing range. I had a blue set of ear protectors, to muffle out the blasts. My father's arms barely flinched when he fired a .45. Standing next to him, I could feel the pressure of the shots on my face. Moving air.

I can paint my father's arms from memory. Stout, brown, covered in black hair. When he took off his gold-colored Seiko, he had a stark tan line on his wrist. His hands were broad, short. He wore a simple gold band that choked his fat finger. He had, not a mole, a black mark of some kind, just below the ring, which he still has today. I was always watching his hands to make sure where they were.

I got tired of the target shooting, too. Dad kept thinking things up. Bought me this Bullworker, showed me how to use it. I got into that for a while. I liked how my body started looking.

The closet in my bedroom had two mirrored doors. I worked out in front of them. Didn't take long to develop at that age. Shirtless, I stared into the mirrors, flexing, tracking my progress. Feeling my arms, my thighs, my stomach, my chest. I measured my waist as it slimmed, my biceps as they grew. I looked for the cleft in my triceps, the ridges in my forearms, the veins popping up. I watched dark hair spread out over my shins and thighs, up from my groin, across my stomach and over my chest. Under my arms.

Dad tried to get me into a lot of things. Soccer, tennis, the Boy Scouts, archery, the weights. Didn't interest me. Usually, just ended up watching TV or reading those Hitchcock books, Horror Stories for Kids.

We dissected a baby pig in biology class.

(Pause.)

Stiff. The skin. Not soft and bendable like living skin. The ears, the snout, even the insides… you'd expect the guts, the stomach, the lungs, the intestines, all of that to be soft. Slick, you know? Tender. But it was dead a long time. The formaldehyde soaks up into everything, drying it like a hard rubber. Even the veins. *There was no blood. A lot of people didn't want to do the dissection. Didn't bother me at all.*

One of the first things I remember . . . we were living out in Ames. For a while, there was a bad smell coming from under the house. My dad went down to the crawl space with a flashlight and a plastic bucket. Started pulling out all these bones. Big pile under there. Small bones. Birds, mice, all kinds of rodents. My dad said it was the civets going down under there to eat their prey, leaving the bones. I was probably four, five.

(He begins to pull out bones and place them on the stage, one by one.)

I found this when I was twelve in a wooded area between

two lots. I think it's a vertebra from a large animal. It's stone now, not bone anymore. It's old. For years, I've been meaning to contact a museum to see if they could figure out what it is. I've even fantasized that it's some rare prehistoric fossil that they'll pay me millions for . . . the missing link . . . and I'll be able to live off it for years. Or I'll donate it and be lauded for my selfless contribution. They'll name a wing of the museum after me. At least a room.

A turtle shell. The underside. Looks like the front end was split off. Or the back end. With a shovel or something. Don't remember where it came from.

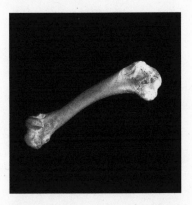

Don't remember this one, either. I think it's a leg bone of some kind. Maybe a cat or a small dog.

(He rattles some small bones in his hand.)

Vertebrae.

(He rattles them again.)

They line up. There are quite a few missing from the full spine. They're light, like they're made of pressed paper.

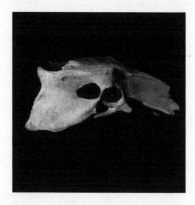

It's a skull. From what, I don't know. Found it out on the road near my house. Brought it home. Put it in an old plastic container with some bleach, just overnight, under my bed, to get anything remaining off it. Any tissue. If my mother had found it … It's not from a cat or a dog or even a raccoon or anything like that. I think it's from a bird, something big … a heron, maybe, which I saw some when I was growing up.

I used to ride around the neighborhood on my bike. Took some garbage bags with me. I looked for animals on the side of the road. Dead ones. I didn't kill them. Cats and dogs, possum, sometimes birds, a snake once. Made a cemetery in back of a neighbor's yard across the street, back in the property, in the woods. Made crosses out of sticks. There was dissection. I don't know what got me started on all this. It's a strange thing to be interested in. There was a dog ... mid-sized, twenty-five, thirty pounds. Used a sharp knife from the kitchen, probably a four-inch blade. Cut from the neck down. Took the guts out, the organs from under the ribs. Doesn't take much to lay it out flat. Broke the ribs, with my hands, snapped them from the sternum. Pulled the legs out of their sockets, nailed them open, the ribs open, the skin and muscles back, the whole body cavity open. Nailed it to a tree. I was gonna skin it, strip the flesh off, bleach the bones, then reconstruct it and sell it. Never got that far. Took the head off. Stuck that on a long stick in the ground. Just as a prank. That was in another neighbor's property a couple of houses down, back in the woods in a depression between some trees. Took a friend back there to see it. Told him I found it. The mouth was a little open.

(He mimics this.)

Freaked him out.

They asked Jeffrey Dahmer's high school teacher what kind of student he was. She said, "He was a real cut up."

His favorite book? *A Farewell to Arms*.

(A sharp light illuminates his hand.)

There are eight small bones in the wrist, four anterior, four posterior. Linate, hamate, capitate, triquetral, scaphoid, trapezium, trapezoid, pisiform. Then five metacarpal bones in the palm, extending to the proximal, middle, and distal phalanges of the fingers. Above the bones are ligaments. The carpal ligaments wrap around the wrist like layers and layers of rubber bands. And there are ligaments around each of the phalangeal joints of the fingers. Above the ligaments are muscles and tendons. Various muscles in the palms and long muscles extending from the forearm ending in long tendons that reach all the way to the tips of the fingers. Sheathes around each segment of each finger hold the tendons in place, like cigar bands. Thick white nerves, like roots, extend from the forearm, running over and under muscles. Then the several layers that make up the skin.

(He makes the following gestures with his hand in the light.)

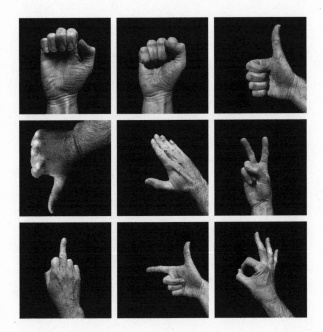

DESIRE/EXILE

Where I grew up, there wasn't anyone. I mean not a single gay person I know of. It wasn't accepted ... at all. So, you know, you get frustrated.

My best friend was a kid lived in the neighborhood.

Jason Corello. Jason Corello's father mowed the lawn shirtless.

(He smiles.)

I used to watch from my bedroom window. Jason and I played sports together across the street from both our houses. Our front-door neighbors were snow birds and their big yards were ours all summer to play tag, hide-and-go-seek. Jason and I played football, two-hand-touch. We played basketball on the street, shooting hoops into a net that a neighbor put up. Playing sports together, Jason and I developed into young men. Lost fat, developed muscles. Beards grew in. Our voices quavered together between high and low before dropping for good. Jason began to work out. He would wear cut-off shirts. I would watch, when he took shots at the net, how his stomach was flatter and the light brown hair was growing around his belly button. I wonder if he ever caught me watching him and, if he did, what he said to himself to convince himself it was all right.

I started having fantasies probably at fifteen. Meeting a good-looking hitchhiker and ... sexually enjoying him. Don't know where the fantasies came from. He'd look like something in a magazine. Jeans. No shirt. Developed arms and chest. Attractive. He'd be on the side of the road. No ride. No money. No one to call. Totally stranded. I'd drive up, ask him if he wanted a lift. I'd take him back home or out in the woods. Same place where I took the animals, where I dissected them. And he wouldn't know where. You know, somewhere in Ohio. I'd have him out there, drunk.

Wesley. A year and a half before graduation. A sleepover at a friend's house. Wesley. His mother was part German, part Iroquois. She had straight, thick hair, but it was almost white. An angular face, high cheeks, green eyes. Strong. Beautiful. Wesley was the same, except with curly hair from his Nordic father. He was slim, sinewy. His face when he smiled ... I didn't know I thought he was beautiful. I didn't know I wanted him. Didn't know it then, when we were seventeen, the only boys at the sleepover. Didn't know it when we lay in the bed together, in the boys bedroom, or when he rolled onto his stomach and I touched his back, his shoulders through the thin, wasted fabric of his ratty old t-shirt. I told him, "These are called the scapula, the deltoids, the biceps, the triceps. Don't know what the forearms are and there are lots of muscles in the hands." He rolled over and took off his shirt and I still didn't know. I didn't know when I combed his hair with my fingers and touched his ears, his face, down his neck. "These are the clavicles, the collar bones. The pecs. The sternum. The ribs. Are you ticklish? The abs."

(He breathes in slowly.)

He sat up and faced me. Took off my shirt, my underwear. I thought I would be with him forever.

For a year and a half, until I left for college, Wesley and I messed around. He would say it was just a phase. Every week or two, just a phase, and I thought it was just a phase for Wesley until he called in the middle of the night my second year of grad school, five years later, to tell me he thought he might be gay. "It's all right, Wes." But not when we were seventeen. I didn't care what he called it. I would drive out to his parents' house on Longboat Key, out over all the bridges . . . to this day the smell of the ocean makes me think of Wes. But sometimes we were at my house. My room just a few steps from the living room, from my father's recliner where he would often fall asleep, snoring to the sounds of an old movie on TV. Behind my closed bedroom door ... Wes and I ... the things we would do. Going through our phase. Not a locked door. We didn't lock doors in my house. My father could have woken up, walked over, turned the knob, and ... So I always listened for his snoring. The things Wesley and I did behind a closed door.

BEHIND CLOSED DOORS

Behind a closed door lies John, waking on a Sunday morning, weak, heavy. There was a battle, there was a fever, there was a binge of drugs. He stands from the edge of his bed, looks in the mirror, knowing why the sheets stick to him, why his arms and chest sting, knowing from the dull weight on his body ... "I lost a lot of blood." Cuts over his ribs. On the undersides of his arms deeper cuts. He'll pick at them daily so they won't heal, bleeding over and over. Johnny's skilled behind closed doors. When the surge of pain wells up ... "it's like a volcano" ... pain that started with his mother, hyper and insane, who abandoned him at ten and a father who expected too much, "fucking prick." So when the lows come they burst like swollen blisters. Out spills the hate, the rage ignites every muscle, and regret like sawdust in his mouth, disgust and shame over every part of his body. Johnny cuts gashes down to the muscle on the undersides of his legs, from his heels to the backs of his knees. He digs a knife so deep into his arm he hits bone. He burns the tips of his fingers so often his fingerprints are spirals, distorted and permanently melting. Johnny's good. He digs a straight razor completely under his skin. He paints with his blood. He eats it. When he's rushed to the emergency room because he cut into an artery, all he thinks about is watching the blood spill out.

"I want out" ... the pain ... "I want it all out." When he sees it go, dripping down his arm to the floor. Quiet. It's gone. There's finally peace.

Behind a closed door Paul stretches out on the couch, his bed, 'cause he's here for the count 'til the alarm goes off. Cushions flat, plaid worn away, a dip where the springs gave up. It's after ten, and the movie's in the VCR like every night. Four pillows crammed in a corner so his head's up. He can't breathe anymore flat. There's a little plastic end table from Walmart right here, the remote, a loaf of white bread, a pound of bacon he fried to the thoughts in his head. "I'm alone. No one loves me. No one will, 'cause I'm so fat. I'm so ugly. I'm so fucking stupid. Why don't you just lose some weight, you fat fuck? What's wrong with you? You're so fucking fat. Who's gonna love you? Who's gonna love you? You fat ass." Paul lives alone behind a closed door, three eighty-five three years ago, last time he checked. He's got *Tootsie* on the tube, his favorite sweats on, the waist giving way, folding bacon into buttered white bread. The whole pound wrapped in the whole loaf. Except two slices for an ice cream sandwich, a real ice cream sandwich with three scoops of soft vanilla ice cream smushed in between. "Lots a people would think it's gross, but it's great." Salty bread against sweet cream. Messy, but who cares? Who?

Blinds drawn. Door locked. Lights off. He pulls up his shirt, sucks up—

(He does this.)

—what's dropped off. Maybe a crumb of bacon, too. The salt shoots through the cream on his tongue. "Unh." He hugs a pillow to his chest. "I'm so alone." Lights out. Passed out. Snoring. He wants to die.

Behind a closed door there's little Carlito, who calls people he doesn't know. Strangers he found on the internet. Numbers he got illicitly. A couple of rings, then, "Hello?" "Hello." "Hello?" "What are you doing? You still in bed?" "No." "You sound tired." "Who is this?" "It's Carlito." Click. "That's okay." Wait for the star sixty-nine. Nothing? He dials again, "Oh, I want to hold your stick in my hand." Click. Wait. Wait. "Call me." Nothing? Dial again. "Ooo, I want you to fuck my hole." Click. One more breath—

(He breathes in orgasm.)

"Oh, baby."

Behind a closed door there's Jeff: tall, lanky, not a man

yet. A year ago, some seniors on the street rushed him and struck him, hard.

Don't know why. Wasn't doing anything. Just come up behind someone and hit 'em.

Hard, with a billy club. But Jeff can't forget. Doesn't know why. For a whole year, it stays in his head.

I thought about it a long time. I guess it made me angry.

This was before the fantasies, picking up hitchhikers. Lonely men, with no way to get to where they want to go. Jeff would pick them up, and the things he would do …

I don't know where it came from.

He tried to stop, later. Went to church with his grandmother. Tried drugs to render lovers insensible.

I didn't want to do it anymore.

He didn't want to do it anymore. He wanted to be somebody he wanted to be. He wanted to be somebody his father wanted him to be. But that was later, not now. Not the young, polite, lanky, strange, quiet boy behind a closed bathroom door, nerves fired, electricity. Booze in his blood. Happening just like the dream.

Just like I dreamed it.

Behind the closed bathroom door, Jeff puts the man's head on the cold tile floor and masturbates over it.

(He breathes in orgasm.)

(Lights shift.)

When I was eighteen, my fantasy happened. I was driving home from a bar. About a mile from my house, there he was. His shirt was off. I was attracted to him. I drove past, then stopped. I had no idea what to do. I pulled back, asked him if he wanted to come over, smoke some pot, and he said, "Oh, yeah." My dad had moved out by then. My mom and little brother were staying at a motel five miles away. We got back, went to my bedroom, had some beers. Didn't take long to figure out he wasn't gay. After a while, he wanted to go. Didn't know how else to keep him there, so I got one of my barbells . . . the rod where you put on the weights . . . hit him . . . on the head. I was working out then. You have to hit hard to knock someone out. His head was bleeding. I got on top of him. Strangled him with the bar.

(He looks down, breathes in.)

I got pretty frightened at what I'd done. Paced around the house. Ends up I did masturbate.

RELIGION/REPRESSION

I was eighteen when I told my mother I wasn't attracted to women. That's how I said it. I remember my sister came in at some point . . . no locked doors in my house. I told her like it was the worst thing in the world, like I was dying. My mother told my father. It was a weeknight, but they took me to see a priest. The drive there, no one said anything. I leaned my head against the window. So ashamed. I remember the rectory. Behind the walls . . . I knew there must be people, but they were so quiet. I heard the footfalls as the priest approached. Clicks on the hard linoleum. My father went first to another room to talk to him. Then they came back for me. I went into a little room with this man I didn't know. He spoke so quietly. He didn't look at me, or I didn't. I don't remember his face. I could hear my father's words in his mouth. "Your dad told me that you said you aren't attracted to women. Is that right? Don't be afraid. Do you touch yourself?" "Yes." "You shouldn't do that. If you stop doing that, everything will be alright." I did look at him then. I couldn't put the thoughts together, but I knew . . . "They can't help me."

That night, I took the body to the crawl space under the house. Tried to sleep down there, but I was too wired.

The next day, he bought a hunting knife and that night he went into the crawl space and cut the abdomen open, masturbated. Cut off the arm, then all the limbs. Into triple-layered garbage bags and onto the back seat of the car. Three A.M. Driving ten miles from his house to throw the pieces into a ravine, a cop stops him out on a back country road.

Gave me the drunk test.

Shined the flashlight onto the back seat. "What's that?"

Garbage. Didn't get a chance to dump it. Even with the smell, and I was terrified, he just gives me a ticket for driving left of center.

Then back home with the remains, back to the crawl space. Next morning, he takes the pieces and stuffs them into a large storm drain buried on a hill in the back of the property.

Then we went off to college.

I drank every day. Sold my blood for money so I could afford the alcohol. I went so often, they put a check next to my name to make sure I didn't get too much blood drained.

I remember when I bonged some wine. Stood on a chair, mocking my voice teacher. "If you can do it, you can do without it, but if you can't do it, well then you're stuck." At Beaux Arts, at the end of every year, Black friends in starched white tutus, à la *Swan Lake*, and Darryl Watts in a silk skirt (nothing underneath), sandals, head shaved, shirtless, eyes made up with thick black liner, like an Egyptian, the queen of the Nile. And Clayton dressed as Jessye Norman. "Ah, I broke a nail." I drank. I looked down Rick Stein's graduation gown (nothing underneath). I kissed a girl, Deb Levesque, a flautist, and we went back to her room and made out. I talked to Wade. "Wade, I just want to tell you two things. First, you are sooo tall. Second...you are so tall." I drank a lot.

Every night. Slept 'til mid-afternoon, missed classes. Failed everything.

A .45 GPA. His highest grade was a B- in riflery.

I didn't know who I was. Every time I slept with a guy, I was petrified. Afraid he'd hurt me. I slept with a few guys. They were all only one night. I was drinking. I didn't remember who they were. Their names, faces. I didn't want to keep doing that.

It was about two and a half years later. The rest of the family was at work. Opened the drainage pipe. Smashed the bones with a sledgehammer. Scattered them in the underbrush. Took the necklace and the bracelets, threw them over a bridge into the river. Burned the clothes. To make a final end of it.

I didn't want to keep doing that.

But I kept drinking. I was arrested.

His father sends him to live with his grandmother in West Allis, a suburb of Wisconsin. He gets a job drawing blood at the Milwaukee Blood Plasma Center. He went to church with his grandmother. Read the Bible. Went to AA meetings. Pushed out any sexual thought at all. Everything was quiet.

Started working nights at the Ambrosia Chocolate Company. Third shift, sleeping days. Everything was quiet.

LOVE/FILLING THE VOID

I told a friend: I feel like a ship, an old wooden ship tied to a dock, pulled by a storm, and all of these sailors, they're ripping up the moorings on the pier, and the ropes are snapping and whipping around, and the boat's being pulled out into the tide. And she said, "Are you the ship or are you the sailors?"

One night, he was sitting in the library, reading. A guy walks up and drops a note in his lap. It reads, "Come down to the lower-level bathroom, and I'll give you a blow job."

This is ridiculous. It would take a lot more than that to . . .

This guy, John. Freshman year, we hung out all the time. He was straight. I wasn't out then, even to myself. I left for summer break early that year. I'd gotten a job at Colorado Shakes, in Boulder, and John was from Denver, so he drove up that summer a few times to see me. I went down to Denver, too.

Went to the doctor. Told him I worked third shift and was having trouble sleeping days, so he gave me some sleeping pills. At the club, I'd go into a room with someone, and I'd already have a drink for them, usually about five pills crushed into it,

which was five times the dosage. Took about thirty minutes for
them to fall asleep and then I could do what I wanted. They'd
wake up in a few hours.

I remember once standing in John's doorway watching him sleep.

But I didn't bring anyone home again.

I found out that after I'd left school for the summer, at the Beaux Arts Festival, in front of the whole school, John and I were voted cutest couple. He was straight. From Denver. When we got back to school for sophomore year, it was different. A girl who was interested in John told him, "Don't you realize he's in love with you?" That was the end of our friendship.

There was another guy, Steve. We were real close, but he freaked when I came out. I asked him, "If you saw me walking across campus holding some guy's hand, what would you do? Would you pretend like you didn't know me? What if I was kissing a guy? What if I touched you?" He said, "I'd hit you. Well, maybe not the first time." That was the end of that friendship.

Every time I got hurt, I'd pull away. From everyone. Friends, family. I couldn't trust anyone. I was really afraid.

I read in the obituaries where an eighteen-year-old boy had died. Went to the viewing. He was attractive. I masturbated in the bathroom. Went to the graveyard at midnight, was going to take the body home.

But the ground was frozen. He robs a mannequin from a department store. His grandmother finds it in his closet, dressed in a shirt and shorts. His father forces him to get rid of it. He gets kicked out of the gay baths.

A man has a wound—

(He holds out the palm of his hand.)

Here. When he grasps what he wants, there's pain. Does he let go? Or does he hold on to what he yearns for regardless of the pain?

There was another John.

This was a nice-looking guy at a bar.

A dancer. Beautiful.

I get us a room at the Ambassador Hotel.

He was straight, and I knew better.

I was drinking 151-proof rum with Coke.

He would ask me to massage him. And I would, for hours.

Made him the drink.

He'd wear these little nylon running shorts and nothing else ... at all.

He fell asleep.

But I wouldn't let myself, I never ... One day ...

I wake up the next morning ...

He tells Darryl and me that he let this guy suck his dick.

And I must have blanked out, 'cause I don't remember anything.

But I still wouldn't. I didn't want to lose our friendship.

47

He's on his back, his head hanging over the bed. My forearms are completely bruised. His ribs are broken and everything. I beat him to death. I had no intention of doing that.

When he realizes that he wants me to ... and that I know he wants me to.

I had no intention of doing anything.

And that was it.

PRELUDE

His grandmother finds a gun under his bed, a .357 Magnum with a two-and-a-half-inch barrel. He tells his father it's a target pistol.

One morning his grandmother is coming down the stairs—

Don't come down! I'm not dressed! I'm not dressed!

Later that day she sees him taking a stumbling man, apparently drunk, to the corner bus stop.

There was a terrible odor in the garage, a garbage pail with black sludge in it. He tells his father he was experimenting with bleaches and muriatic acid on chicken parts from the grocery store and later a raccoon he finds on the side of the road.

His father: "Why would you be adding chemicals to these things?"

Just to experiment.

"But what kind of experiment, Jeff?"

Just an experiment, to see what would happen.

"But what would be the point of that?"

I know it's stupid, Dad, I just like to experiment.

His father thought it all had to do with the alcoholism.

Images come into my head. Myself as an infant, in a diaper, on the floor. There's a whirlwind of activity around me. Legs passing, this way and that. There's yelling. I don't understand. I reach up, but no one sees me.

I remember playing a board game with my father, and my sister contradicts him. They go back and forth, and I remember thinking, "Stop, stop, it's gonna happen." And he explodes. He throws the game board across the room. His voice is on fire. I don't know what happens next, because my arms cover my face.

I remember my father saying, "If you ever … I'll kill you."

I moved out of the house, after six years. I needed my own space.

The Oxford Apartments on North 25th Street, Apartment 213.

Why did Jeffrey Dahmer need to find a new apartment?
He needed more elbow room.

DEATH/KEEPING

Alfred Hitchcock's *Torn Curtain*, with Paul Newman and Julie Andrews: there's a scene where Hitchcock shows how hard it is to kill someone. East Germany, behind the Iron Curtain. Newman, an American agent, is followed into a farmhouse by a German spy. When Newman and the farmer's wife realize that the spy has found them out and is placing a call to the authorities, a ten-minute murder sequence begins. And there's a taxi driver waiting outside the house, so the killing must occur in complete silence—no guns. The farmer's wife hurls a pot of boiling soup at the spy, then pulls the phone cord out of the wall as Newman puts the spy in a headlock and gets rid of his gun. Then the wife picks up a huge kitchen knife and stabs the spy while Newman restrains him . . . the blade snaps, lodging in his chest. But he's still alive, and Newman still has him pinned. So she gets a large shovel from the corner and swings . . . three hard blows to the head. The spy goes down, but he's still alive. He gets up, opens the window to holler out to the taxi driver. When Newman tries to stop him, the spy begins to choke him. The farmer's wife looks around the kitchen for something else. Finally, she turns on the gas in the oven, and she and Newman—who's still being strangled and on the verge of passing out—they drag the spy across the kitchen floor, placing his head into the oven. The final moments, we watch the spy's hands loosen from around Newman's neck. They dance frantically, struggling, grasping to free himself . . . until they go limp.

I chose men from the neighborhood who were on foot. No cars to trace.

He offered them fifty dollars to go back to his apartment and pose for photographs. If they were attractive enough to keep, he would make them the drink. Entertain them until they passed out.

I wanted to make it as painless as possible.

He would pose them. Take photographs. Have sex with them. He always wore a condom. Then strangle them with a leather strap. More sex. More photographs.

I would sometimes go down to Chicago for the weekend, meet a guy and invite him to come back up with me.

He kept parts of their bodies.

I didn't want it to seem like such a waste.

Steven Hicks was the hitchhiker, the first guy.

> (After speaking the name of each victim, he
> holds up the victim's picture.)

Scared the hell out of me.

This is a mixtape that Wes made for me. He gave it to me
the last day I saw him before leaving for college. It's heavy
metal. Wes was in a heavy metal band.

Then there was the guy at the Ambassador Hotel eight
years later: Steven Tuomi.

> (He searches for something.)

This was from John, the first guy I really loved.

(He cannot find it.)

I don't have anything from him. The bastard never gave me anything.

I had no intention of doing that.

And there were two in Grandma's basement: James Doxtator and Richard Guerrero.

This was from an acting teacher. At the time, I wished this teacher had been my father.

While out on bail, awaiting sentencing for molesting a Laotian youth, he killed Anthony Sears, cut off his head and kept it in a small, locked wooden box.

I was totally out of control.

There were Raymond Smith, Edward Smith, Ernest Miller.

It took about two hours to dismember and get rid of the body. Messy. In the bathtub. Flesh down the toilet. Never clogged it once.

This was from the other John. A sandalwood necklace. The carved beads in the medallion roll around. John brought it back from a tour in India. Sent me a postcard, telling me, "You should really see this," and about how he had to duck to enter the Taj Mahal, because the door was so short.

David Thomas, Curtis Straughter.

This was my first actual boyfriend. He's standing on top of a glacier in Iceland. I put away all of his pictures after we broke up, except for this one. I just couldn't. It made me smile. Which I hated.

Konerak Sinthasomphone, Matt Turner. He tried to make them zombies. Drilled into their heads and poured a mild acid into the hole. He didn't know Konerak was the older brother of the Laotian boy he had molested three years earlier.

What are the chances of that?

Once, there was eating of flesh.

Wanted to make them a part of me.

What did Jeffrey Dahmer tell guests arriving late for a dinner party? "Sorry you couldn't be here earlier—everyone's eaten."

He picked up Jeremiah Weinberger in Chicago.

The apartment manager came in several times because of the smell, but he said it was his freezer had gone on the blitz or that the smell was coming from his fish tank.

(He chortles.)

He believed it.

What were Jeffrey Dahmer's favorite foods? Elbow macaroni. Hand burger.

Errol Lindsey.

Butt steak. Peter bread.

Anthony Hughes.

Finger sandwiches. Head cheese.

Oliver Lacy.

Manwiches.

The apartment manager found a plastic trash can in the closet with acid in it to get rid of what he didn't want to keep. When the manager opened the lid, he almost passed out from the smell. He told him it was full of old water from the fish tank.

(He chortles.)

He believed it.

Joseph Bradehoft was the seventeenth.

This was given to me by a man I loved for thirteen years. For a short time we were lovers. He was straight.

(He makes a cutting motion across his abdomen.)

There's really a lot more to say about him, but ...

I always tried not to get to know the person too well.

He was the last one.

HEAVEN

How does the soul leave a drugged and strangled body?
Does it know? Awake while the body sleeps, then is murdered, seeing it all happen? Does it float out gently, rising
up toward the heavens? Or is murder a surprise?

(He breathes in.)

Is the spirit pried loose, forced to wake, propelled away
from a familiar, comfortable place and compelled by something it doesn't want, forced by a stronger power, a tidal
pull or the gravity of planets holding the universe somewhat in place? Does the soul know where to go? Does it
push and kick and stretch to find a way out, not because it
wants to, but because it must? Where it resided so long is
burning and rotting, while something else, the undertow,
dragging it off its feet, a clumsy, desperate struggle, pulled
under? Is the soul finally ripped out an orifice—the eyes,
the anus, the nose, or out the ear like blood? When it is
drawn up—struggling arms, hands grasping at air, trying
to hold on to the body it loves, fighting and frightened
of what pulls it away—does the soul look back to itself,
its body as it's drawn up, and see the man bending over
him . . . a quick breath in—

(He breathes in.)

He killed me. Does the spirit finally wake, give up its struggle, and mourn ... not looking back nor towards the frightening place where it is going? It's over.

The summer after my junior year, I had an internship at the Goodman Theatre in Chicago. I roomed with two friends on Elaine Place, a one-block street at the epicenter of the gay Mecca of the Midwest, between Halsted and Broadway and Cornelia and Roscoe. Officially named Lakeview, we called it Boystown. A block from my house was the strip of gay bars: Roscoe's, Sidetrack, Gentry, the Cell Block, Circuit, Spin, Charlie's, Buddies, Little Jim's, the Lucky Horseshoe, Cocktail, the Manhole. The bars were filled with tall Aryan boys, blonde, blue-eyed, corn-fed boys who flocked to Chicago from less tolerant neighboring states ... Iowa and Illinois, Kentucky and Ohio, and Wisconsin.

Hey.

Hey.

What's your name?

Ignacio.

What?

Ignacio.

Ignatzio?

Ignacio. What's your name?

Jeff.

Hey.

You're not here all alone are you?

Believe it or not.

My lucky night. What do you do?

I'm an actor.

Yeah?

I'm going to school.

Wow. So you wanna be on Broadway?

Uh. That's a long way off. What do you do?

Nothing that exciting. I work in a factory.

Doing what?

A mixer. I mix chocolate. Exciting, huh?

I love chocolate.

I also take pictures, on the side.

Yeah? You're a photographer?

Well, that's a long way off.

(They chuckle.)

I'd like to take your picture.

(IGNACIO laughs, embarrassed, shy.)

I'm serious. Want to come over to my place? I'll take off your clothes and take pictures of you. What do you think?

(IGNACIO is embarrassed.)

Ah, my God.

(Pause.)

Let me buy you a drink, and you can think about it.

(Pause.)

You don't have to buy me a drink.

(Blackout. A quick breath in.)

End of Play.

AUTHOR'S NOTE

It's easy to understand Jeffrey Dahmer's infamy. Since that summer day in 1991 when his private obsessions became public perversions, he's been a symbol for depravity and degeneracy. A monster. Inhuman.

Everyone knows who Jeffrey Dahmer was . . . at least, everyone my age does. In 1991, stories about him took over the local and national news. I have little doubt he was a hot topic during water cooler conversations, in living rooms, and at dinner tables across the country. In subsequent years, books about him appeared, as well as magazine articles, even a graphic novel. His father wrote a moving, almost confessional account of his son's life. Documentaries and television specials about him were broadcast, screened, and streamed. Even a film based on the graphic novel received wide release. To this day, you can easily find online Dahmer's prison interview with Stone Phillips, recorded just a few months before Dahmer himself was murdered.

The grotesque, perverse nature of Dahmer's crimes brought him infamy. But it wasn't a sordid craving on our part, I don't believe, that drove us to learn more about him. It was our desire to understand how anyone could do what he did. We saw him as a monster. But he was also a man. It's that tension between inhumanity and humanness that we want to reconcile.

When I began thinking about the piece that eventually became *Severed*, Dahmer wasn't on my mind. What started it all for me were some questions I couldn't stop asking: What are the limits of empathy? What is the nature of forgiveness? How do we know when we've paid for our crimes? What does justice really look like and how do we know when it's been realized?

Initially, I began looking at historical figures that could serve as dramatic vehicles to explore these questions. Hitler came to mind first. But, perhaps because I'm gay and perhaps because I was in my early twenties—still an impressionable age—when Dahmer became part of the national zeitgeist, he soon became my focus.

I began to learn more about him. I read his father's book, which was deeply saddening. The more I discovered, the more some shocking realizations came into focus: not only was Dahmer a real, breathing human being, but, even more troubling for me, he and I shared some similarities in our childhoods. I think those realizations hooked me

and made me want to examine his story, as I understood
it, in my play.

That affinity between my childhood and Dahmer's opened
up a door, a sliver of empathy in me. Of course, his crimes
disturbed and sickened me. But always, in the back of my
mind, I could never shake the simple understanding that,
at one point in our developments at least, he and I shared
something. It was easy to condemn him for what he did,
but at one time he was a confused, troubled gay kid, just
like me. So, I was never at liberty to judge him without
some strings attached. That tension between empathy and
judgment only grew in me as I wrote *Severed*.

Some time ago, I was working on a reading of *Severed*.
During those evening rehearsals, I was often alone in a
semi-dark theater, on stage with just the work lights on.
I'm somewhat embarrassed to admit it, but there were
times during those rehearsals, after working on a section
or two, that I'd look out into the audience, and it was as if
I could feel someone…listening…as if some essence of
Dahmer was in the theater with me. I tried to ignore it,
because I knew it was ridiculous, a creation of my over-
active imagination. I'd plow on with rehearsal. But once
the rehearsal was over and I was back out on the street,
I'd think back on those moments, when I imagined that

I was alone in a room with some essence of Dahmer. It was nothing less than chilling. But I eventually felt something else, too, once I'd moved beyond the childish unease. During that time on stage, as I was trying to walk in Dahmer's shoes, the energy I felt was not that of a monster, but of a deeply troubled person. And I also felt a sense of gratitude, gratitude from him that someone was considering his experience with even an ounce of empathy.

In the end, I came to feel about Dahmer much the way I felt about him after reading his father's book: profoundly saddened to recognize such a damaged and damaging life. Perhaps, ultimately, it is that sadness that eclipses everything else, because I don't think the tug of war between empathy and judgment, for Dahmer, can ever be resolved. At least, not in my mind.

One other thing about the whole process of researching, writing, and rehearsing *Severed* still troubles me: some unresolved questions. Why test my theories on the limits of empathy on someone like Dahmer? Why add to his infamy? What about the seventeen young men Dahmer tortured, murdered, and mutilated? I'm sure their family members and friends would have a few choice words for someone trying to find empathy for a man who destroyed so many lives.

In response, I have only a weak defense: the deaths of these seventeen young men offer no gray areas, no room for doubt, no confusing dichotomies. These men died horrible deaths, and their bodies were desecrated. Their families suffered what no family should suffer. When it comes to explorations of empathy and justice, their stories hold no unanswered questions, only very clear answers. They didn't deserve any of it. They only deserve our deepest empathy. And if my work should ever come to add to anyone's pain, I heartily apologize.

I will also add a final thought, and it's something that became clearer to me as I worked on this piece. There is a lot to be gained from looking at another person's life, a person who did so many unconscionable things, and challenging ourselves not to dismiss it outright. Labeling him as unnatural, inhuman . . . that seems a little bit like an easy way out. I can't help but feel that it lets us off the hook in some way.

Because, in the end, Jeffrey Dahmer wasn't a monster. He was a human being. And I believe, buried within the nightmare of his life and acts, there's a rare opportunity to deepen our own humanity by considering his more fully.

-Ignacio Lopez

PRODUCTION NOTE

One of the seminal visual images in the development of *Severed* was Jeffrey Dahmer's prison interview with reporter Stone Phillips. This image may be useful to those staging this work, as the prison setting can help to delineate the performance space. For example, positioning Dahmer behind a clear partition during some of the action can suggest the type of partitions found in prisons, which separate inmates from visitors, while, at the same time, creating discrete playing spaces. This partition can also add an interesting tension to the performer/audience relationship. In addition, anchoring the play's setting to a specific time and place can help draw the audience's attention to character psychology and relationships, thematic issues, and other elements, and away from trying to decipher where the play's action is taking place.

AFTERWORD

Of the seventeen men that Jeffrey Dahmer murdered and mutilated, fourteen were people of color. Nine were Black. Four were under eighteen, including the fourteen-year-old Konerak Sinthasomphone, a Laotian immigrant who escaped from Dahmer's apartment and was discovered—naked, drugged, and bleeding—by three Black women who called the police and prevented his recapture. When the two white police officers arrived, they disregarded the women's testimony and Sinthasomphone's obvious distress. They took Sinthasomphone back to Dahmer's apartment, where he was murdered later that day.

The racism displayed by these officers is appalling, almost incomprehensible. But *abhorrent* is not the same as *aberrant*: the officers, like Dahmer, acted in accordance with racist and homophobic systems that remain in place today. The murder of Black, brown, Indigenous, and immigrant people by U.S. police and security forces is not only not aberrant, it is essential to what policing is and has always been, as we can see by the blatant, brutal murders committed by police officers like Derek Chauvin, Jonathan Mattingly, Brett Hankison, and Myles Cosgrove, as well as by federal troops, ICE, and the DHS, among others. Dahmer's monstrosities were continuous with and made possible by systems of legal violence and injustice that make some people more believable and more grievable than others.

It is in this sense not only an act of empathy to recognize that Dahmer was not a monster. It is also a recognition that the systems that produced him are the systems we learn to live and love within. We are implicated. In setting his own biography alongside Dahmer's, and in tracing with deep vulnerability and terrifying tenderness the echoes between their two lives, Ignacio Lopez invites us to consider the ways in which our own acts of love, pleasure, and care are shaped by structures of violence, capitalism, and white supremacy.

Lopez's rigorous exercise in empathy ought to invite our very strict interrogation of how violence, hate, and fear can become internalized; how trauma can be transposed into violence; and how the living forces of slavery, colonialism, and capitalism can sicken our acts of love and desire, turning them into expressions of ownership and power.

The specificity of Lopez's reckoning with a life so near and yet so far from his own ought to inspire our most passionate and detailed accounting of all that we must abolish in order to live and love differently. What systems of care, support, art, and imagination might alter the course of a life, might let our love at last be loving?

-Kate Kremer

ACKNOWLEDGMENTS

My gratitude goes out to Jim Nicola, Linda Chapman, and the artistic staff at New York Theatre Workshop for supporting my creations over the years, including the very first iteration of *Severed*, and for giving me the space to explore. This play would not be what it is today without Noel Allain, John Del Gaudio, William Burke, and everyone at the Bushwick Starr, who brought this piece to new life. A special thank you to Jillian Walker for spurring my creative courage and for opening doors to new opportunities. Kate Kremer's enthusiasm for *Severed*, for which I am immensely grateful, gave birth to this publication. Finally, I would not be who I am today without Jim Colleran and Jenny Simon, who have unfailingly nurtured and championed me as an artist and as a person.

CONTRIBUTORS

Ignacio Lopez is a playwright and performer living in Brooklyn, New York. His work has been supported by New York Theatre Workshop, the Bushwick Starr, and INTAR Hispanic American Arts Center. He has contributed his writing, dramaturgical, and performance talents at the Public Theatre, the Goodman Theatre, the Williamstown Theater Festival, Northlight Theatre, Victory Gardens Theater, and the Colorado Shakespeare Festival.

Noel Allain is the Founding Artistic Director of The Bushwick Starr Theater. He is a graduate of Skidmore College and the Juilliard School's Drama Division. As an actor, he has performed in various theater, television, and film productions in and out of New York City. At the Starr, he has programmed artists and companies such as Heather Christian, Jeremy O. Harris, Dave Malloy, Half Straddle, Daniel Fish, Clare Barron, Ayesha Jordan, The Mad Ones, Phillip Howze, Erin Markey, David Greenspan, Haruna Lee, Diana Oh, and Jillian Walker. He has developed the Starr's workshop, Creating Performance, in collaboration with El Puente Leadership Academy, and its after school program, Big Green Theater, with Superhero Clubhouse. He has served as a panelist for NYSCA, LMCC, The Shed, Sundance Theater Lab, and

HERE's HARP Residency; appeared as a guest artist for the University of Iowa's New Play Festival; and as a guest speaker at Colombia, NYU, Hunter, Bard, Skidmore, and the Prelude Festival.

Kate Kremer is a playwright and the editor of 53rd State Press.

ALSO FROM 53rd STATE PRESS

The 53rd State Occasional No. 2 // Ed. Will Arbery
Suicide Forest // Haruna Lee
Rude Mechs' Lipstick Traces // Lana Lesley + the Rude Mechs
MILTON // PearlDamour
The People's Republic of Valerie, Living Room Edition // Kristen Kosmas
Uncollected Trash Collection // Kate Kremer
A Discourse on Method // David Levine + Shonni Enelow
Severed // Ignacio Lopez

FORTHCOMING
Ann, Fran, and Mary Ann // Erin Courtney
I Understand Everything Better // David Neumann + Sibyl Kempson
ASTRS // Karinne Keithley Syers
Wood Calls Out to Wood // Corinne Donly
Love Like Light // Daniel Alexander Jones
WATER SPORTS; or insignificant white boys // Jeremy O. Harris
12 *Shouts to the Ten Forgotten Heavens: Springs* // Sibyl Kempson

53rd State Press
new writing for performance

Book design: Kate Kremer
Interior images: Ignacio Lopez
Cover design: Vind Datter

53rd State Press publishes lucid, challenging, and lively new writing for performance. Our catalog includes new plays as well as scores and notations for interdisciplinary performance, graphic adaptations, and essays on theater and dance.

53rd State Press was founded in 2007 by Karinne Keithley in response to the bounty of new writing in the downtown New York community that was not available except in the occasional reading or short-lived performance. In 2010, Antje Oegel joined her as a co-editor. In 2017, Kate Kremer took on the leadership of the volunteer editorial collective.

For more information or to order books, please visit 53rdstatepress.org.

53rd State Press books are represented to the trade by TCG (Theatre Communications Group). TCG books are exclusively distributed to the book trade by Consortium Book Sales and Distribution, an Ingram Brand.

Severed is made possible by the New York State Council on the Arts with the support of Governor Andrew M. Cuomo and the New York State Legislature.